DAD JOKES

THE PUNNY EDITION

First published in Great Britain in
2021 by Cassell, an imprint of
Octopus Publishing Group Ltd
Carmelite House
50 Victoria Embankment
London EC4Y 0DZ
www.octopusbooks.co.uk

An Hachette UK Company
www.hachette.co.uk

Copyright © Octopus Publishing
Group Ltd 2021
Text Copyright © Kit Chilvers 2021

Distributed in the US by
Hachette Book Group
1290 Avenue of the Americas
4th and 5th Floors, New York,
NY 10104

Distributed in Canada by
Canadian Manda Group
664 Annette St., Toronto,
Ontario, Canada M6S 2C8

Kit Chilvers asserts the moral
right to be identified as the author
of this work.

ISBN 978 1 78840 257 6

A CIP catalogue record for
this book is available from the
British Library.

Printed and bound in the UK

10 9 8 7 6 5 4 3 2 1

Publisher: Stephanie Jackson
Editorial Assistant: George Brooker
Designer: The Oak Studio
Deputy Art Director: Jaz Bahra
Production Controller: Serena
   Savini

This FSC® label means that
materials used for this product
have been responsibly sourced.

MIX
Paper from
responsible sources
FSC® C104740
FSC
www.fsc.org

DAD JOKES

JOKES

THE PUNNY EDITION

Kit & Andrew Chilvers

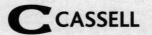

**Dedicated to Ollie Thomas –
without him, none of this would
be possible. Thanks, Ollie.**

Introduction

Hello again, fellow jokesters.

Yes, it's another year and yet another *Dad Jokes* book. Let all your friends and family know they need to try this new one on for sighs.

As usual, thanks to our ever-growing community of jolly japesters on Twitter, Instagram and Facebook for their incisive wit and savage rejoinders. Your engaging banter is often far funnier than the jokes themselves, so please keep those comments coming.

It's been a tough year, and laughter has never been more important.

Lots of love as always,

Kit & Andrew

Ten plus ten and eleven plus eleven both equal the same number.

Ten plus ten equals twenty, and eleven plus eleven equals twenty, too!

_____

What's the leading cause of dry skin?

Towels.

What do you call a dead magician?

An abra-cadaver.

I was arrested yesterday after neighbours complained about me playing Engelbert Humperdinck records all night.

Police released me, let me go!

What is the hardest cult to join?

The diffi-cult.

———————

I had a vasectomy because I didn't want any kids.

But when I got home, they were still there.

I told my psychologist I am scared
of living in a tall building.

He said it's only an apartment complex.

What do you call a Viking who doesn't
draw much attention to himself?

Low Key.

I hope Elon Musk never gets caught up in a scandal.

Elon-gate would be really drawn out.

Please, you have to stop making police-related puns.

OK . . . I'll give it arrest.

I hired a handy man and gave him a list of things to do. At the end of the day, only items one, three and five were done.

It turns out he only does odd jobs.

_____

Did you hear about the poker player who broke his arm?

He's finding it hard to deal with.

I can't understand why my calculator stopped working.

It just doesn't add up.

_____

Two antennas got married . . .
The ceremony was OK, but the reception was excellent.

If a woman says she'll be ready in 15 minutes, she will be.

There's no need to remind her every half hour.

———

I could never date a kleptomaniac.

I don't think I have what it takes.

I just got fired. As severance, my company gave me a bag of used coffee.

They said it was grounds for termination.

What did Arnold Schwarzenegger say to his tomato seeds after they started growing into plants?

You have been germinated.

Congratulations to me! I just made my last mortgage payment.

I still owe about $262,000, but I'm just not going pay them anymore.

————————

As I was getting into bed, she said: "You're drunk."

"How do you know?" I asked.

She said: "You live next door."

I made a pencil with
two erasers today.

It was pointless.

I would like to go to Holland someday.

Wooden shoe?

———————

A detective showed up at my house and asked me where I was between five and six.

I told him I was at school.

I asked an electrician to fix an electrical issue at my house.

She refused.

_____

My girlfriend told me that I'm pretty.

Well, the whole sentence was, "You're pretty annoying", but I try to focus on the positive things.

Why didn't they let the fungi
into the party?

There wasn't mush room.

———————

Did you know that Spiderman has
a winter jacket made entirely of
Mediterranean flatbread?

It's a pita parka.

I can't find my cake anywhere.

It was stollen.

_____

I tried to warn my son about the dangers of Russian roulette.

But it went in one ear and out the other.

What is the best type of cheese
for disguising a horse?

Mascarpone.

_____

I got a hammer lodged in my
oesophagus and the doctors can't
remove it.

They say it's the worst case of a
Thor throat they've ever seen.

Why do astronauts use Linux?

Because they can't open Windows.

I don't mean to brag, but yesterday
I beat our local chess champion in
less than five moves.

Finally, I was able to put my high-school
karate lessons to some use.

What do you call two birds stuck together?

Velcrows.

Scientists just discovered a new, cow-like plant.

They're calling it a bo-vine.

What did Newton think when he discovered gravity?

"Sh*t is about to go down."

My favourite schoolteacher was
Mrs Turtle.

Strange name, but she tortoise well.

———————

Sales are down, so my boss asked why
the greeting cards aren't moving.

I told him it's because
they are stationary.

I've got the body of a porn star.

All my clothes say "XXX".

_____

The recipe said: "Set the oven
to 180 degrees."

Well, now I can't open it because
the door is facing the wall.

Everyone was
excited at the
Autopsy Club.

It was open
Mike night.

Today, my wife apologized for the first time ever.

She said she's sorry she ever married me.

———————

I've just realized it's Pancake Day.

That really crêped up on me.

Does every sentence need to include a vegetable?

Not necces-celery.

———

In my job interview, they asked me about my best qualities.

"Well," I said, "my doctor always calls me patient."

My wife and I just celebrated ten years of happy marriage.

It was, coincidentally, our 30th wedding anniversary.

_____

Does anyone want my old copies of *Chiropractor Monthly*?

I've got loads of back issues.

What did one boob say to another?

"If we don't get support, they'll think we're nuts."

If you spell the words "absolutely nothing" backwards, you get "gnihton yletulosba".

Which, ironically, means . . . absolutely nothing.

If Mary is the mother of Jesus, and Jesus is the lamb of God, does that mean that Mary had a little lamb?

———————

My English friend was really proud of his heritage until he found out that his great-grandfather was from Transylvania.

Now he can't even look at himself in the mirror.

I know two spiders who recently got married and bought their first home together.

I am so happy for the newlywebs.

_____

What do you call a wizard who walks everywhere on bare feet, has poor bone density and is cursed with really bad breath?

A super-calloused fragile mystic hexed by halitosis.

I hate how funerals
are always held
at 9am.

I'm not really a
mourning person.

Today I learned that if you're in a canoe and it flips over in the water, you can safely wear it on your head.

Because it's capsized.

———————

I once swallowed a book of synonyms.

It gave me thesaurus throat I've ever had.

My wife asked me today if I had seen the dog bowl.

I said no. I didn't even know he could.

My wife thinks we should allow our pets to share our bed, so I agreed.

After ten minutes of flapping about, the goldfish finally settled down.

I recently bought 51 per cent of a vampire-hunting company.

It means I'm the main stake holder.

———————

My buddy keeps asking me to blow cool air on him when he gets hot, but I don't like it.

I'm not a fan.

I don't understand the science behind human cloning.

That makes two of us.

My wife asked me to put ketchup
on the shopping list.

Now I can't read it.

———

Yesterday, I went rock climbing and
the guy above me kept farting.

It was by far the worst ass-scent
I've ever had to deal with.

What pronouns does a chocolate bar use?

Her/she.

How do ghosts listen to music?

With boo-tooth.

Why did the cyborg have to rest after his long road trip?

Because he had a hard drive.

Are people born with a
photographic memory?

Or does it take time to develop?

_____

What did Spartacus say when the
lion ate his wife?

Nothing – he was gladiator.

My wife and I are finally fulfilling my lifelong dream of visiting the Golden Gate Bridge.

"What are you going to do when you finally get there?" she asked.

I said: "I'll cross that bridge when I come to it."

What do you call someone who points out the obvious?

Someone who points out the obvious.

There's a snowstorm warning in
Wall Street.

What a terrible time for shorts.

———————

What do you call a deer in a downpour?

A raindeer.

At the end of the physics lecture,
I asked my professor: "What happened
before the Big Bang?"

He said: "Sorry. No time."

————————

I'm always Frank with my
sexual partners.

I don't want them to know my
real name.

I've offered my elderly neighbour $20 to let me try out her stair lift.

I think she's going to take me up on it.

––––––––––––

My girlfriend says if we don't get married soon, she's gonna kill me.

It's a matter of wife or death.

A dung beetle walks into a bar and asks: "Is this stool taken?"

How does a computer get drunk?

It takes screenshots.

_____

Today I found out that you can actually _hear_ the blood flowing through your veins.

You just have to listen varicosely.

Finally, my winter fat has gone.

Now, I have spring rolls.

I just figured out why Teslas
are so expensive.

It's because they charge a lot.

I had to fire the guy I hired to
mow my lawn.

He just didn't cut it.

————————

My wife told me I've really grown
as a person.

Her actual words were "You've got fat",
but I know what she meant.

You need to do more chores around the house.

Can we change the subject?

OK. More chores around the house need to be done by you.

Why don't professional boxers have sex before a fight?

They probably don't fancy each other.

_____

When my wife found me playing with my son's train set, I was so embarrassed that I threw a bedsheet over it.

I think I managed to cover my tracks.

Is my wife dissatisfied with my body?

A tiny part of me says yes.

Can anybody give me some advice
on how to remove the ice from
my windshield?

I just tried using a discount card I had
in my pocket, but I only got
20 per cent off.

Why did the cows return to the
marijuana field?

It was the pot calling the cattle back.

What do you call a sleeping dad?

Anything you want – he can't hear you!

_____

**Yesterday, I got into a heated argument
with a snowman.**

**He lost his cool and had a
total meltdown.**

There's something that I don't like about "DO NOT TOUCH" signs.

I just can't put my finger on it.

———————

I asked the hot dog seller: "Can I get a jumbo sausage?"

"Sure," he said. "It won't be long."

"In that case," I said, "can I have two?"

I told my therapist I can't get the *Grease* soundtrack out of my head.

He said: "Tell me more."

My farmer friend used his government grant to buy baby chickens.

He got the money for nothing, and the chicks for free.

_____

If I'm reading their lips correctly . . .

. . . my neighbours are arguing about some creepy guy next door.

How did Kim Kardashian tell her kid about her upcoming divorce from Kanye?

"North, things between West and I have gone south."

———

People call me self-centred.

But that's enough about them.

Why is moon rock tastier than
earth rock?

It's a little meteor.

_____

My GPS just told me to turn around.

Now I can't see where I'm driving.

I visited my friend at his new house. He told me to make myself at home.

So I threw him out. I hate visitors.

Yesterday, one of my good friends told me I often make people uncomfortable by violating their personal space.

It was a really hurtful thing to say and completely ruined our bath together.

———————

Is "butt cheeks" one word?

Or should I spread them apart?

I arrived at the restaurant early.
The manager said: "Do you mind
waiting a bit?"

"No," I said.

"Great," he said. "Take these drinks
to table nine."

_____

What starts with a W and ends with a T.

It really does, I swear.

Some people these days are
too judgemental.

I can tell just by looking at them.

———————

Personally, I think that beekeeper suits
are ugly as hell, but hey.

Beauty is in the eye of the bee-holder.

I bought coconut shampoo today.

But when I got home, I realized
I don't even have a coconut.

_____

Lance is quite an uncommon
name nowadays.

But in medieval times, people were
called Lance a lot.

Which tree wishes things were more like they used to be?

Pine.

I gave my French girlfriend a pendant engraved with the words "Le monde".

It means the world to her.

———————

I broke up with my girlfriend of five years because I found out she was a communist.

I should have known – there were red flags everywhere.

What do you call James Bond taking a bath?

Bubble 07.

What's the difference between a dog and a marine biologist?

One wags a tail, and the other tags a whale.

My daughter told me she saw a deer on the way to school.

I said: "How do you know it was going to school?"

Daddy, do all fairy tales start with "Once upon a time"?

No, dear. There's a whole series of fairy tales that start with: "If elected, I promise . . ."

**What do you call a dinosaur
that crashes his car?**

Tyrannosaurus Wrecks.

_____

It hurts me to say this, but . . .

. . . I have a sore throat.

Every day, I come home and ask my dog how his day was, and every day he gives the same answer:

"Ruff."

_____

What did Mariah Carey say when her boyfriend bought her an undeveloped patch of land so they could build their dream house?

"I don't want a lot for Christmas."

My wife keeps telling me I am of average intelligence.

Now that's just mean.

_____

What do you call an animal that knows if you're lying?

A sealion.

I once entered the Kleptomaniac
World Championships.

I took gold, silver and bronze.

_____

My partner always makes such a mess
when cooking her breakfast, but I'm
terrified of asking her to clean up.

I've been walking on eggshells all day.

I accidentally put
Viagra in my ear.

Now I'm hard
of hearing.

What did the dad say to his son when he became afraid of the full moon?

"Don't worry! It's just a phase it's going through."

———

Someone removed the fifth month from all my calendars.

I am really dismayed.

What do you call the pink fleshy bits between a shark's teeth?

Slow swimmers.

What should you use with Batman shampoo?

Conditioner Gordon.

I ordered a second-hand deck of cards from a casino, but after four weeks, they still hadn't been delivered, so I called them up to see what was going on.

Turns out, they were still dealing with my order.

What does the electrician say when he meditates?

"Ohm."

I had the nastiest, rudest and slowest cashier at the supermarket today.

I guess it's my own fault for using the self-service checkout.

———

I saw a guy walk into a store and buy five smoke machines, so I called the police.

He must be in some extreme-mist group.

My kid refuses to eat fish. What do you think would be a good replacement?

Try cats. They love fish.

I have a friend who writes songs about sewing machines.

He's a Singer songwriter, or sew it seams.

No matter where I go, I like to bring my ukulele.

That way, whenever someone asks if I play an instrument, I can say: "I play a little guitar."

Dear Optimist, Pessimist and Realist,

While you were arguing about the glass of water, I drank it.

Sincerely,

Opportunist

99.9 per cent of people are dumb.

Fortunately, I belong to the 1 per cent made up of smart people.

_____

I told my wife I'm going to arrange the herbs in alphabetical order from now on.

"Where would you find the time?" she asked.

I said: "Easy. Right next to the sage."

What happens when you drive
a Subaru in reverse?

Ur a bus.

———————

A police officer stopped me
and demanded I get out of the car.
"You're staggering," he said.

"Well, thank you," I replied.
"You're not so bad yourself."

I visited a monastery the other day, and as I walked past the kitchen, I saw a man frying chips.

I asked him: "Are you the friar?"

He replied: "No – I'm the chip monk."

What musical genre are national anthems?

Country.

Did you hear about the depressed ghost?

He's going through some things.

A piece of macaroni, a piece of penne and a stick of spaghetti were drinking wine in a bar one evening. They saw a noodle sitting by himself and discussed inviting him to join them.

They all agreed he looked cannelloni.

———————

An armed man runs into a real estate agency and shouts: "Nobody move!"

What do you call an alligator attorney?

A litigator.

———

Amal and Juan are identical twins. Their mother only carries one baby photo in her wallet.

If you've seen Juan, you've seen Amal.

A man arrested for being drunk
wakes up in a cell.

"Why am I here, officer?" he asks.

"For drinking," replies the cop.

"Great," says the man.
"When do we start?"

_____

What language do doctors curse in?

Ibuprofane.

It's a shame nothing is made in this country anymore. I just bought a TV and the box said: "Built in antenna."

To be perfectly honest, I don't even know where that is!

———

When I moved into my new igloo, my friends threw me a surprise house-warming party.

Now I'm homeless.

Me: Your underwear is far too tight and very revealing.

My wife: Wear your own then.

I caught my dog chewing on my boots yesterday.

I guess he has really good taste in footwear.

I asked a librarian if they had any books on different noise levels.

The librarian said: "Yes, we have several. Which volume would you like?"

———

Why did the non-binary prospector head out west?

Because there was gold in them/their hills!

My boss asked me why I only get sick on workdays.

I said it must be my weekend immune system.

_____

I'm done being a people-pleaser . . . if everyone's OK with that, I mean.

**You really should try archery
while blindfolded.**

You don't know what you're missing.

_____

**What do you call two guys holding
up drapes in a window?**

Kurt and Rod.

What do you call a typo on a headstone?

A grave mistake.

_____

My Russian friend told me that the best part about being Russian is getting to vote in American elections.

Which is nice, because he never gets to vote in his own.

I went on a date last night with a woman I met at the zoo.

It was great – she's a keeper.

———————

My boss came to me at lunchtime and said: "Where the hell have you been? I've been looking for you all morning!"

I shrugged and said: "Good employees are hard to find."

I've never been married . . .

. . . but I've had a few near Mrs.

My wife threatened to divorce me when I said I was going to give our newborn daughter a silly name.

So I called her Bluff.

———————

One sloth turned to the other and said: "I never used to like moss, but now it's starting to grow on me."

What part of the hospital has the least privacy?

The ICU.

_____

I quit my job at the concrete plant.

My work was getting harder and harder.

Ancient Egyptian architect: "Do you know how to build a pyramid?"

Ancient Egyptian builder: "Well, um, yeah . . . up to a point."

———————

At my boss's funeral, I leaned down and whispered to the coffin: "Who's thinking outside the box now, Gary?"

Doctor: Can we talk about your weight?

Patient: Certainly. It was about 20 minutes – but at least the chairs didn't break this time.

When facing a bear attack recently, I accidentally played "dad" instead of "dead".

Now it can ride a bike without stabilizers.

———————

A buddy of mine named his dog "Five Miles" so he could tell people he regularly walked five miles.

But today, he ran over Five Miles.

I ate a kid's meal at McDonald's today.

His mother got really angry.

This morning, I accidentally put Red Bull in my coffee maker instead of water.

I was halfway to work before I realized I'd forgotten my car.

My son might not be the best roofer in the world . . .

. . . but he is up there.

My wife and I share the same sense of humour.

We have to – she doesn't have one.

———————

Last week, I built a model of Mount Everest.

My son asked: "Is it to scale?"

"No," I replied. "It's to look at."

The swordfish has no natural predators to fear . . .

. . . except the penfish, which is said to be even mightier.

———————

What do you call a home for lopsided horses?

Unstable.

Did you fog up the bathroom mirror again?

I can't see myself doing that.

You may think it's funny to kiss someone while you have a runny nose.

But it's snot.

———————

The mayor in my city just passed a law saying that male best friends have to have lunch together at least once a week.

Well, it's not a law. It's a mandate.

You shouldn't throw
sodium chloride
at people.

That's a salt.

Whenever my artist girlfriend is sad,
I let her draw things on my body.

I give her a shoulder to crayon.

_____

I have a friend with no social skills and
a PhD in the history of palindromes.

I call him Dr Awkward.

A fortune-teller told me that, in 12 years' time, I'd suffer terrible heartbreak.

So, to cheer myself up, I bought a puppy.

_____

Midwives deserve a lot of respect.

They really help people out.

My wife insisted on pouring flour into the melted butter.

I told her she would roux the day.

———————

Do they allow loud laughing in Hawaii?

Or do you just stick with a low ha?

At my book club, I wondered why they were throwing Stephen King novels around.

Then *IT* hit me!

My wife asked for a divorce today, saying I was too un-American.

I saw it coming from a kilometre away.

Dad: Go to bed, the cows are sleeping in the field.

Daughter: What's that got to do with anything?

Dad: It means it's pasture bedtime.

What do you call a person who eats other people slowly?

A cannibble.

―――――――

I've been trying to play the new official Rick Astley board game.

But the instructions just say: "You know the rules, and so do I."

The worst pub I've ever been to was called The Fiddle.

It was a vile inn.

If anyone is alone this Christmas and has nobody to spend it with, please let me know.

I really need to borrow some chairs.

I wanted to become a professional fisherman . . .

. . . but I discovered that I couldn't live on my net income.

My sister just delivered a baby.

I knew she had it in her.

_____

My husband decided to take the elevator, whereas I chose to go for the stairs.

I guess we were just raised differently.

What does a CIA agent do when it's time for bed?

He goes undercover.

I read a study the other day claiming that humans eat more bananas than monkeys.

Which – to me – sounded a bit obvious. I mean, I can't remember the last time I ate a monkey.

My son accidentally smashed his foot on the table leg.

As he was hopping around the room screaming in pain, I rushed to the phone, picked it up and asked him: "Do you want me to call . . . a TOE TRUCK?"

———————

I hurt my bottom after shaking it at the office party.

It was a twerk-place injury.

I've been trying to convince my dad to get a new hearing aid.

But he just won't listen.

I know a lot of jokes in sign language, and I can guarantee you no one has ever heard them.

———

My wife won't let me get a tattoo of a grizzly on each bicep.

She is infringing on my right to bear arms.

I saw a man going up a hill with a trolley full of horseshoes, four-leaf clovers and rabbits' feet.

I thought: "Wow, he's pushing his luck!"

————————

What do you call a sad robot?

A sigh-borg.

What washes up on the shores of small beaches?

Microwaves.

_____

I've just heard that, by law, you have to turn on your headlights when it's raining in Sweden.

How the hell am I supposed to know when it's raining in Sweden?

Someone just called my phone, sneezed and hung up.

I am getting sick and tired of these cold calls.

———————

If a pig loses its voice . . .

. . . does it become disgruntled?

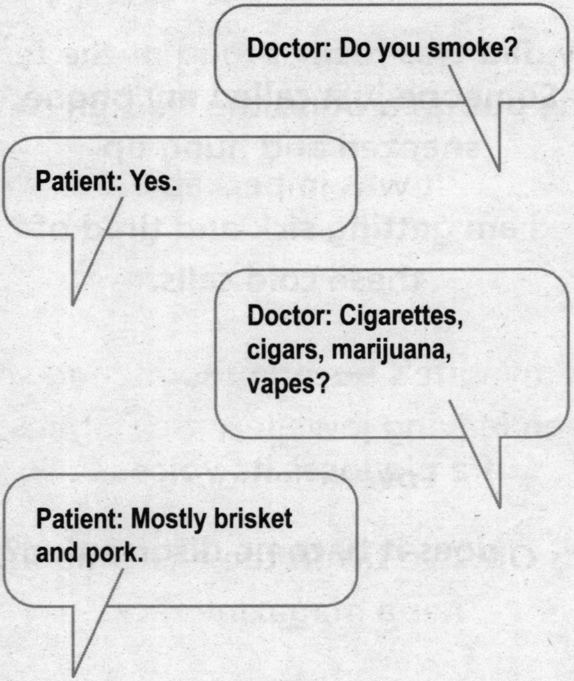
Doctor: Do you smoke?
Patient: Yes.
Doctor: Cigarettes, cigars, marijuana, vapes?
Patient: Mostly brisket and pork.

My dad was really proud of the fence he put up around the chicken run.

It was impeckable.

———————

It's my wife's birthday soon, and she's been leaving jewellery catalogues all over the house.

It's OK, I've taken the hint: I bought her a magazine rack.

What do you
call a detective
electrician?

Sherlock Ohms.

Imagine if Americans switched from using pounds to kilograms overnight.

There would be mass confusion.

After playing guitar for years, I thought I could learn to play the piano.

But it's not an easy instrument to pick up.

When ordering food at a restaurant, I asked the waiter how they prepare their chicken.

"We don't do anything special," he explained. "We just tell them they're going to die."

_____

What part of the body always loses?

Defeat.

I married my wife for her looks . . .

. . . but not the ones she's been giving me lately.

I was at the store with my wife picking out a turkey and she seemed unimpressed by the size.

She asked: "Don't they get any bigger?"

I looked her in the eyes and replied: "No honey. They're dead."

To kill a French vampire, you have to drive a baguette through its heart.

It sounds easy enough, but the process is *pain*-staking.

My uncle smokes. He also loves David Bowie.

We call him Ciggy Stardust.

What do you get if you cross an angry sheep with an disgruntled cow?

Two animals in a *baa*d *moo*d.

_____

Dwayne Johnson's downstairs neighbours are clueless about almost everything.

I suppose you would be, too, if you lived under a Rock.

My grandma is
80 per cent Irish.

People call her Iris.

A group of bottoms is out for a hike. The smallest struggles to keep up.

"Sorry," it says. "I'm a little behind."

_____

Last night, as I lay in bed gazing up at the stars, I thought: "Wait – where the hell is my roof?"

What is the only four-letter
sport that starts with a T?

Golf.

_____

Why did the wizard's wife have love
bites on her neck?

Because he was a neck-romancer.

Iamonthemoonandthereisnowhereto-getabeer.

Thereisnospacebar.

_____

I'm really upset because I just got my doctor's test results.

It turns out I'm not going to be a doctor.

Gravity is one of the most powerful forces in the universe.

But without it, you still have gravy.

_____

I had an industrial accident last week – I fell into an upholstery machine.

I'm fully recovered now.

My grandad used to say: "If it wasn't for me, you'd all be speaking German right now."

He was a lovely man, but a terrible languages teacher. I have no idea why the school hired him.

———————

An epidemiologist, a scientist and a doctor walk into a bar.

Just kidding – they know better.

Why don't monsters eat ghosts?

Because they taste like sheet.

_____

What's worse than biting into an apple and finding a worm?

Biting into an apple and finding half a worm.

Me: Help me doctor,
I'm shrinking!

Doctor: OK, calm down.
You'll just have to learn
to be a little patient.

Today, I opened
my very own
pizza restaurant.

I will be rolling in
dough in no time.

What's made of leather and sounds like a sneeze?

A shoe.

People often say that most women want to get married, but I don't think that's true.

I've asked loads, and they've all said no.

My wife says she's thinking of leaving me because of my obsession with poker.

I think she's bluffing.

————

Why is spicy food like a credit card?

You pay for it the next day.

We should thank heaven for nipples.

Without them, boobs would
be pointless.

_____

I accidentally parked in a "Reserved
for witches" spot.

When I got back, there was a
note on my windshield that said:
"You will be toad."

I can't tell you the whole of Japanese history in one sentence . . .

. . . but I can samurais.

_____

I've decided to quit my job as a personal trainer because I'm not big enough or strong enough.

I've just handed in my too-weak notice.

Genie: I shall grant you three wishes.

Me: I wish for a world with no lawyers.

Genie: Done. You have no more wishes.

Me: But you said I could have three!

Genie: Sue me.

My wife is kicking me out because she's fed up with all my South American animal puns.

"OK," I said. "Alpaca my bags."

Have you heard about the artist who uses different types of steak to create portraits of people?

A rare medium, but well done.

I was on the beach and got hit by a massive wave of cake.

It was a tiramisu-nami.

———————

How can a room full of married people be empty?

Because there's not a single person there.

I cut my birthday cake in half and ate both sides.

I wanted to halve my cake and eat it too.

———————

My wife just yelled that I should "fall in a pit or hole sunk into the earth to reach a supply of water and die".

I know she really means well.

What's it called when you kill chickpeas?

Hummus-ide.

Did you hear about the zombie bodybuilder who hurt his back?

He was dead-lifting.

———————

Two cats had a swimming race. One cat was called "One Two Three", and the other was called "Un Deux Trois". Which cat won?

One Two Three – because Un Deux Trois cat sank.

I knocked up my ex-girlfriend.

Although I'm being told that's not how I should announce my wife's pregnancy.

———

Bilbo Baggins was caught by surprise by someone singing "Don't Stop Believing".

It was An Unexpected Journey.

What did the prawn say to the scallop at the party?

"I think I've pulled a mussel!"

———————

I'm going to open a takeaway cheese shop.

I'll call it "Whey to Go".

What did the church mouse say to the other mice?

"Have you accepted cheeses as your Lord and Saviour?"

———————

A man walks into a sperm bank.

The doctor says: "Would you get a load of this guy?"

I watched a film about graphs, but it was really disappointing.

The plot was predictable, and the special f(x) was terrible.

_____

Why was the baby strawberry crying?

Because its parents were in a jam.

My grandfather always said: "Fight fire with fire."

He was a great person, but a terrible fireman.

I entered my chihuahua in an "ugliest dog" contest and won first place!

My dog came third.

_____

I tried to visit the house where the guy who invented toothpaste was born.

Sadly, there was no plaque on it.

Did you hear about the man who only collected rare pennies?

He didn't have a lot of common cents.

_____

I have never owned or used a telescope in my life, but it's something I'm thinking of looking into.

A friend asked me: "As a little boy, was your mum super-strict with you?"

I said: "My mum was never a little boy."

———

A tub of margarine fell on my foot three weeks ago and it still hurts.

I can't believe it's not better.

What do you call a half-man, half-horse who always hogs the limelight?

The centaur of attention.

_____

If a tree falls in the forest and no one is around to hear it . . .

. . . then my illegal logging business is a success.

My family thought of me as a failure.
Then I invented an invisibility cloak.

If only they could see me now.

———————

Why shouldn't you let your kid become
a musician?

There's too much sax and violins.

Why are demons fat?

Because they hate exorcising.

I was wondering why there are so many stories about vampires in Europe, but not in Africa. Then I remembered that vampires are killed by holy water.

And they bless the rains down in Africa.

———————

I was riding a donkey the other day when someone threw a rock at me and I fell off.

I guess I was stoned off my ass.

If it seems like everything is going
your way . . .

. . . you're probably in the wrong lane.

———————

Where do cow farts come from?

The dairy air.

Every time I go to the liquor store,
a dude comes out of nowhere to give
me advice on what to buy.

I like to think of him as my spirit guide.

———————

My bartender friend broke up with
her boyfriend . . .

. . . but he kept asking her for
another shot.

I got a vinyl album of wasp sounds the other day, but when I played it, didn't sound anything like wasps.

Then I realized I was listening to the bee side.

_____

What is a sea monster's favourite food?

Fish and ships.

I don't mean to brag, but . . .

. . . cashiers are *always* checking me out.

It's pretty obvious that if you run *in front* of a moving car, you will get tired.

But if you run behind it, do you just get exhausted?

———

I just found out my toaster wasn't waterproof.

I was shocked.

This morning, my car was completely covered in fallen leaves.

You could call it an autumn-mobile.

———————

Why shouldn't you kiss anyone on 1st January?

Because it's only the first date.

My son told me he can drink a whole glass of whiskey straight.

Personally, I think it's neat.

———————

What's the longest word in the English language?

Smiles. The first and last letters are a mile apart.

I invented a car that only moves when the driver is silent.

It goes without saying.

My partner dumped me for only talking about video games.

I said: "What did we have to *Fallout 4*?"

Ever since I killed one of my chickens with the lawnmower, all manner of scary, haunting things are happening to me.

I think I may have a poultry-geist.

My teenage daughter can't decide whether she wants to be a hairdresser or a short-story writer.

I guess she'll have to flip a coin to help her choose: heads or tales.

_____

You could say I have an hourglass figure.

It takes me an hour to figure out where my glasses are.

I bought a chicken to make a sandwich.

Turns out it just poops all over the floor – and doesn't know how to make sandwiches.

———————

My medieval servant is missing, so I tried to look him up on the internet.

The search engine result said: "Page not found".

A word of advice: don't try to eat
the chickens in *Minecraft*.

They're too gamey.

————————

Freddie Mercury, Bruno Mars and Venus
Williams all walk into the same bar.

But they didn't planet that way.

There's an ancient Neolithic monument dedicated to dad jokes.

It's called Groanhenge.

———

What's the German word for bra?

Stoppemfrumfloppen.

My email password got hacked *again.*

That's the third time I've had to rename the cat.

———————

What do you call a large bird of prey that's unwell?

Illegal.

The first annual meeting of the Camouflage Club was a disaster.

It looked like no one showed up.

Light travels faster than sound.

That's why some people appear bright – until you hear them speak.

―――――――――

After the pandemic, I'm thinking of opening a bar where everyone insults everyone else while moving to the music.

I think my idea of social diss-dancing would go over well!

Did you hear about the watchmaker who is half Spanish and half Irish?

His name is Juan O'Clock.

My pet frog broke his leg this morning.

He's very unhoppy.

Why did the Viking buy an old boat?

He couldn't a fjord a new one.

————

I just got offered a job teaching creative writing in prison.

I spent all night thinking about the prose and cons.

A bossy man goes into a bar.

He orders everyone a round.

———————

Did you hear about the chemist who froze himself to -273.15°C?

Everyone called him crazy, but personally, I think he was 0K.

We all know Sin City is Las Vegas, but do you know what Den City is?

Mass over volume.

———————

I just dropped my phone in the bath.

Now it's syncing.

It takes five minutes to walk from my house to the bar, but 45 minutes to walk back again.

The difference is staggering.

———————

What do you call a person missing 75 per cent of their spine?

A quarterback.

My wife rang me and said: "If you're not home in ten minutes, I'm giving your dinner to the dog."

I raced home in five minutes. The poor dog doesn't deserve that.

———————

My friend worked at the zoo.
His job was to circumcise the elephants.
The pay was bad, but . . .

. . . the tips were huge.

I was out hiking yesterday when I suddenly saw a cougar.

It almost made me puma pants.

———————

After all my plants fell victim to disease this year, I've decided to give up vegetable gardening and become a music producer instead.

I've got a ton of sick beets.

Why are snakes
measured in inches?

Because they don't
have any feet.

Why do golf announcers whisper?

Because they don't want to wake up
the people watching.

What rock group has four members,
but none of them sing?

Mount Rushmore.

The weirdest summer job I have ever had was cleaning the monkey cages at our local zoo.

That sh*t was bananas.

What do you call a Satanist who only eats low-carb pizza?

The anti-crust.

My wife claims that she can wax my chest hair without me feeling any pain.

I just don't think she'll be able to pull it off.

_____

What do you call a bearded vase-maker?

Hairy potter.

I recently found out that Bill Nye is just a stage name.

His real name is William New Year's Eve.

————————

The last thing my grandfather said to me before he died was: "Pints! Gallons! Litres!"

That spoke volumes.

My wife stormed into the pub last night as me and the boys were downing shots of tequila.

"You're coming home right now!" she shouted.

I laughed and said: "No, I'm not."

"Not you," she said. "I'm talking to the kids."

———

What do polar bears and plumbers have in common?

They both want a good seal.

Can you help me out? I'm stuck on this crossword clue: "Overworked postman".

Sure. How many letters?

Well, I'm guessing too many.

What do you call a fish wearing a tie?

Sofishticated.

_____

I like to imagine that the guy who invented the umbrella was going to call it the "brella".

But he hesitated.

Why is nostalgia like grammar?

We find the present tense and the past perfect.

———————

I got a new pair of gloves today, but they're both "lefts".

On the one hand, it's great, but on the other, it's just not right.

If Watson
isn't the most
famous doctor . . .

. . . then Who is.

My left knee has never committed
a crime.

I can't say the same for his felony.

———————

I was recently burgled. They took
my life jacket, my defibrillator and
my portable oxygen tank.

It was my entire life savings.

People overcome adversity all the time. I mean, just look at Beethoven.

They told him he was deaf, but did he listen?

———————

Times New Roman, Arial and Comic Sans walk into a bar.

Before they can even order a drink, the bartender yells: "Get out – we don't serve your type here!"

How does a penguin build a house?

Igloos it together.

_____

The owner of the tuxedo store kept hovering over me when I was browsing, so I asked him to leave me alone.

He said: "Fine. Suit yourself."

Think about it: if you buy a bigger bed, you have more bed room . . .

. . . but less bedroom.

———————

Where's the best place in America to shop for a football kit?

New Jersey.

I quit my job as a
treadmill tester.

I just felt like
I wasn't going
anywhere.

How do you make three old ladies all yell profanities at the same time?

Tell a fourth one to yell "BINGO!"

If I was being subjective, I would have to say that the greatest sci-fi show of all time is *Dr Who*.

If I was being objective, I would say it's *Dr Whom*.

Two cowboys are lost in the desert. One cowboy sees a tree that's draped in bacon.

"A bacon tree, we're saved!" he says. He runs towards the tree – and is immediately shot dead.

It wasn't a bacon tree. It was a ham bush.

_____

My friend works in IT.

I asked him: "How do you make a motherboard?"

He said: "I usually tell her about my job."

I was flattered when I heard they'd made a movie all about my hair.

It's called *50 Shades of Grey*.

What do you call a doctor who is half-man and half-horse?

A centaur for disease control.

I accidentally sprayed deodorant into my mouth.

Now when I talk, I have this weird Axe scent.

_____

I caught my son chewing on electrical cords, so I had to ground him.

He's doing better currently, and is now conducting himself properly.

I'm studying chemistry, and I just learned that sulphuric acid should never be left in a metal beaker.

It's just an oxidant waiting to happen.

———————

Bing Crosby was great, but imagine how good Google Crosby would have been.

Like most people my age, I'm 50.

_____

There are four stages of life, and they all involve Santa.

1. You believe in Santa.

2. You don't believe in Santa.

3. You _are_ Santa.

4. You look like Santa.

My wife told me: "Don't get upset if people call you fat. You're much bigger than that."

Her: Let's try something different. Undress me with your words.

Me: I just saw a spider go into your bra.

A giant fly is attacking the local police force.

They have called for assistance from the SWAT team.

———————

After I was arrested, my ex-wife decided to hang a picture of my mugshot on the wall in her living room.

But she still won't admit she framed me.

I accidentally put my wallet in the freezer last night.

It turned out to be a good thing, though. I really needed some cold, hard cash.

What do you call a bedpan in Russia?

A poo-tin.

I've been working really hard on my spelling lately.

My teacher says I'm almost their.

My wife says I'm addicted to auctions. but she's wrong.

I actually stopped after going once . . . going twice . . .

———————

I have just released my own fragrance.

The people sitting near me on the bus don't look like they appreciate it, though.

They say childbirth is the most painful thing someone can experience.

Maybe I was too young to remember, but I don't think it hurt *that* much.

———————

A penguin walks into an airport.

The security officer stops him and says: "Sorry pal. Penguins can't fly."

WARNING: There is an email going around offering processed pork, gelatine and salt in a can.

If you get this email, DO NOT open it. It's spam.

What's the worst thing about eating a clock?

Passing the time.

My neighbour blamed my gravel for making him fall . . .

. . . but it was his own dumb asphalt.

My friend called me for help, claiming he had turned into a harp.

I raced over there only to find out he was a lyre.

_____

Today I discovered a loophole while wearing my face mask.

It goes around the ear.

Why do lions only mate in the summer?

Because the pride comes before the fall.

———

**What is a web developer's favourite
kind of tea?**

URL Grey.

Max the camel walks into his parents'
room at 2am and asks for a glass
of water.

His dad says: "Another one? That's the
second glass this month."

_____

I bought a new shrub trimmer today.

"Check this out!" I said proudly,
showing it to my son.

"That's great, Dad," he said.

"It's not just great," I said.
"It's cutting-hedge technology!"

**Why are larger penguins
so popular at parties?**

They can really break the ice.

Why didn't four ask out five?

Because he was two squared.

What do you get when you cross a policeman with a skunk?

Law and odour.

_____

Yesterday, I read an article about the dangers of drinking too much.

It scared the hell out of me, so I've decided that from now on, I'm never reading it again.

I took my pet fish to the chip shop
with me the other day.

I asked the man behind the counter:
"Do you do fish cakes?"

He said: "Yep, we do."

"Good," I said, holding up my pet.
"Because it's his birthday tomorrow."

A group of leprechauns was recently
busted for selling fake granite.

Yeah, that's right: they were sham rocks.

Almost all garden gnomes have red hats.

It's a little-gnome fact.

What did the cheese say to itself in the mirror?

"Halloumi."

_____

My wife said that if I don't get off the computer, she'll slam my head on the keyboard . . .

. . . but I think she's jokinfjreoiwjrtwe 4to8rkljreun8f4ny84c8y4t58lym4wthy lmhawt4mylt4amla.

I went to a deli and said: "Hi, I'd like to buy a bagel with cream cheese."

The kid behind the counter said: "Sorry, we only take cash or credit card."

If you've got bladder problems . . .

. . . urine trouble.

My wife and I were having this huge argument about whose turn it was to do laundry.

Eventually, I threw in the towel.

———————

I'm writing a book about hurricanes and tornadoes.

It's only a draft at the moment.

I'd like to thank Merriam-Webster for teaching me the meaning of the word "plethora".

It really means a lot.

I hate it when people get angry
with me for being lazy.

It's not like I've done anything.

————————

A guy stopped me in the street the
other day to ask why I was carrying
a 2-metre book.

I said: "Well, it's a long story."

Some people always need their opinions validated.

Am I right?

_____

Walking home last night, I passed a slice of apple pie, an ice-cream sundae and a lemon cheesecake.

I thought to myself: "Wow. The streets seem strangely desserted."

What do you call an espresso with a cold?

Cough-ee.

_____

On the first day of my diet, I removed all the fattening food from the house.

It was delicious.

Fun fact: Australia's biggest export is boomerangs.

They're also the country's biggest import.

Robin: The Batmobile isn't starting!

Batman: That's strange. Did you check the battery?

Robin: What the hell is a tery?

My wife was upstairs. She shouted down to me, asking: "Do you ever get a shooting pain across your body, like someone's got a voodoo doll of you and they're stabbing it?"

"No . . ." I replied

There was a pause, and then she said: "How about now?"

What did Yoda say when he saw himself on a 4K TV?

"HDMI."

What do you call an angry counsellor?

A therapissed.

I once tied my dog's stick to a balloon, and he brought it back from several miles away.

I know, it sounds a bit far-fetched.

Why did the small pepper wear
a sweater?

It was a little chilli.

_____

I was really excited when my wife
bought me a book for my birthday
called *69 Mating Positions*.

Turns out it's about chess strategies.

What did the instructor at the school for kamikaze pilots say to his students?

"Watch closely. I'm only going to do this once."

_____

I knew a guy who was told he was the worst Best Man ever.

He was speechless.

Someone asked me to name two structures that hold water.

I was like, "Well, damn."

My wife bought me a pet pug as a present.

Despite the squashed nose, bulging eyes and rolls of fat, the dog seems to really like me.

———————

A Tibetan monk saw the face of Jesus in a tub of margarine.

He raised his eyes to the heavens and said: "I can't believe it's not Buddha!"

Kid: Dad, can we get some pets?

Dad: No. Pets are just a step backwards.

Where do rabbits go after they get married?

On a bunny-moon.

_____

Why is it impossible to starve in the desert?

Because of all the sand which is there.

My therapist just told me I have extreme difficulty when it comes to picking up social cues.

I think she is in love with me.

———————

"I have a split personality," said Tom, being Frank.

My horse has insomnia and keeps everyone awake.

She's a total nightmare.

———————

My massage therapist just got fired.

I guess she rubbed too many people up the wrong way.

How do you let birds know when you've refilled the bird feeder?

Send a tweet.

———————

I was surprised when my dad told me he's a retired dog walker.

I'm sure he could walk working dogs, too.

It takes guts to be an organ donor – and balls to be a sperm donor.

If two drug dealers start a relationship, is that considered speed dating? Or are they just meth-ing around?

Where are dead computer hackers buried?

In decrypt.

Did you know that there are no canaries in the Canary Islands?

The same thing applies to the Virgin Islands – there are no canaries there, either.

———————

I was dreaming about having diarrhoea, and then I woke up.

That's when sh*t got real.

What's Dracula's favourite type of coffee?

Decoffinated.

Today, I got a new job working in an elevator.

It's OK. It has its ups and downs.

What did 50 Cent do when he got hungry?

58.

I didn't realize the reopening of the Lego store was going to be so popular.

People were queuing up for blocks.

_____

What do you call an apology written in dots and dashes?

Remorse code.

My wife said that she thinks quilts are better than duvets.

I told her to be careful when making blanket statements like that.

———

I tried to use the army toilets, but one of the officers stopped me and said, "It'll cost you $10 to go in there."

I'm the loo tenant.

My new girlfriend told me I'm terrible in bed.

I told her it's unfair to make a judgement in less than a minute.

What do you call a girl who refuses to pay her bills?

Burnadebt.

Why is the forest so noisy?

The trees bark.

As a doctor, I would never make a joke about an unvaccinated baby.

But, hey – let me give it a shot.

———————

What kind of magic does a condiment wizard perform?

Saucery.

My wife asked me to prepare our four-year-old son for his first day at school.

So I stole his lunch.

_____

What did the lawyer name his daughter?

Sue.

Which country is filled with very bad singers?

Singapore.

_____

My friend bought a bull from the Himalayas that refuses to stand up.

I always see Himalayan there.

What do you call polite houses?

Manors.

**Why wasn't Cinderella allowed
to play soccer?**

**Because she kept running away
from the ball.**

Call me cynical, but I think Orion's Belt
is just a big waist of space.

———————

My wife just threw away my favourite
herb, and now I have to go
and buy more.

I can't believe she'd waste my thyme
like that.

What did the cannibal choose as his last meal?

Five guys.

_____

We have a strict hierarchy policy for PPE usage at my office.

Workers must use face shields. Managers get to use the super-visors.

What beef only comes in 2, 3, 5, 7 or 11-ounce portions?

Prime rib.

_____

My friend's wife is leaving him because of his obsession with barbecues. He's devastated.

He told me: "I'd walk over hot coals for that woman."

Well, Einstein finally finished his theory of relativity.

It's about time.

The only thing I really have planned for today is to get my new glasses.

Then I'll see what happens.

———————

What do you call someone who cleans a Hoover?

A vacuum cleaner.

What do you know about bonsai trees?

Very little.

@DadSaysJokes is a community-run dad jokes network on Instagram, Facebook and Twitter, with over 3 million followers, inspired by the daily jokes of author Kit Chilvers' dad, Andrew.

Every day, followers submit their jokes and the team picks their favourites – or Dad just drops in his own zinger!

Kit, a young social networking influencer, started his career at the tender age of 14, when he created his original platform, Football.Newz. He has since added another nine platforms, including @PubityPets and monster meme page @Pubity, which has over 28 million followers.

Also available:

 @DadSaysJokes

 @Dadsaysjokes

@DadSaysJokes